Animal Spikes and Spines

Antlers

Rebecca Rissman

Heinemann Library
Chicago, Illinois

www.heinemannraintree.com
Visit our website to find out
more information about
Heinemann-Raintree books.

To order:
☎ Phone 888-454-2279
🖳 Visit www.heinemannraintree.com
to browse our catalog and order online.

© 2011 Heinemann Library
an imprint of Capstone Global Library, LLC
Chicago, Illinois

Edited by Rebecca Rissman, Dan Nunn
  and Sian Smith
Designed by Joanna Hinton-Malivoire
Picture research by Tracy Cummins
Production by Victoria Fitzgerald
Originated by Capstone Global Library Ltd
Printed and bound in China by Leo Paper Products Ltd

15 14 13 12 11
10 9 8 7 6 5 4 3 2 1

Library of Congress Cataloging-in-Publication Data
Rissman, Rebecca.
  Antlers / Rebecca Rissman.—1st ed.
    p. cm.—(Animal spikes and spines)
  Includes bibliographical references and index.
  ISBN 978-1-4329-5037-8 (hc)—ISBN 978-1-4329-5044-6 (pb)
1. Antlers—Juvenile literature. I. Title.
  QL942.R57 2012
  599.63'147—dc22   2010044789

Acknowledgments
We would like to thank the following for permission to reproduce
photographs: FLPA pp **11** & **22** (both Terry Whittaker); Getty
Images pp **7** (Ryan McGinnis), **9** & **10** (both James Hager), **15** &
16 (both Shin Yoshino), **23a** (James Hager), **23b** (Shin Yoshino);
istockphoto pp **6** (© James Galpin), **8** (© Mooneydriver); National
Geographic Stock pp **5** (Alaska Stock Images), **17** & **18** (both
Maria Stenzel); Photo Researchers, Inc. p **12** (Kenneth W. Fink);
Shutterstock pp **4** (© Igor Janicek), **13** & **14** (both © Caleb
Foster), **20** (© Susan Chiang), **21** (© Sisters and best friends).

Cover photograph of a bull moose swimming in a pond in Alaska,
reproduced with permission of National Geographic Stock (Alaska
Stock Images). Back cover photograph of a deer reproduced with
permission of istockphoto (© James Galpin).

We would like to thank Michael Bright, Nancy Harris, Dee Reid,
and Diana Bentley for their assistance in the preparation of
this book.

Every effort has been made to contact copyright holders of
material reproduced in this book. Any omissions will be rectified in
subsequent printings if notice is given to the publisher.

Contents

Animal Body Parts

Animals have different body parts.

antlers

Some animals have antlers.

What Are Antlers?

Antlers are body parts.

Antlers grow from animals' heads.

Antlers are made of bone.

Different Antlers

Antlers can be different shapes and sizes.

Antlers can be long and pointed.
What animal is this?

This animal is an elk. It grows new
antlers every year.

Antlers can be short and spiky.
What animal is this?

This animal is a pudu. Its antlers are about the size of your middle finger.

Antlers can be wide and curved.

What animal is this?

This animal is a moose. Its antlers help it to hear quiet sounds!

prongs

Antlers can have many prongs.
What animal is this?

This animal is a reindeer. It uses its antlers to fight other reindeer.

Antlers can be V-shaped.

What animal is this?

This animal is a huemul. Only male huemuls grow antlers.

Your Body

Do you have antlers?

No! Humans do not have antlers.

Humans grow hair on their heads.

Can You Remember?

Which animal's antlers are about the size of your middle finger?

Picture Glossary

 **antler** hard, bony body part grown by some animals. Antlers grow from animals' heads.

 **prong** thin, pointy shape. Forks have prongs.

Index

Notes for Parents and Teachers

Before reading

Create a KWL chart about antlers. On chart paper, make three columns and label them: "K - What do you know?," "W - What do you want to know?", and "L - What did you learn?". Show the children the front cover of the book. Ask them what they know about antlers. Fill in the K column of the chart together. Ask the children what they would like to know about antlers. Fill in the W section of the chart together.

After reading

• Fill out the remaining section of the KWL chart with the children. Ask them "What did you learn?" and add this information in the L column.

• Were there things that the children wanted to know about antlers which were not covered in the book? Discuss this with the children and ask them to suggest ways they can find out more.

24

Note for p18: A huemul is a type of deer.